BULLYPROOF
Unleash the Hero Inside Your Kid

BULLYPROOF
Unleash the Hero Inside Your Kid
VOLUME 6

CONTRIBUTING AUTHORS:
FREDDY BASANTES
CAROL CHAPMAN
J.P. DO
LUIS JIMENEZ
MICHAEL KEENAN
KENNETH MACKENZIE
JOHNNIE MORRIS
LISA PIPER
SHARON RUECKERT
STAN TABOR
KIMBERLY TANNY

EDITORS:
ALEX CHANGHO & KASEY THORNTON

BULLYPROOF
Unleash the Hero Inside Your Kid
Volume 6

Copyright © 2017 Bullyproof America, Inc.

All Rights Reserved. No part of this publication may be reproduced in any form or by any means, including scanning, photocopying, or otherwise without prior written permission of the copyright holder.

DEDICATION

A big thanks goes out to everyone who has supported the BULLYPROOF series and projects around the country and worldwide. It's because of your help that we can achieve our mission to transform kids into heroes every single day.

Thank you.

TABLE OF CONTENTS

Chapter 1: Confidence First – Stan Tabor, Michael Keenan & Freddy Basantes Jr. 1

Chapter 2: Peace Through Defense – Kenneth MacKenzie 13

Chapter 3: Learning to Add with Black Belt Math – Sharon Rueckert 29

Chapter 4: It Takes a Village... to End Bullying – Kimberly Tanny 45

Chapter 5: "Just Ignore It" And Other Myths – Carol Chapman 53

Chapter 6: Different Problems, Different Solutions – J.P. Do 63

Chapter 7: Make Superheroes, Not Victims – Luis Jimenez 73

Chapter 8: The Minecraft Lessons – Lisa Piper 83

Chapter 9: Being Proactive and Getting Educated – Johnnie Morris 99

Getting Involved With The Bullyproof Project 107

CHAPTER 1: CONFIDENCE FIRST

BY STAN TABOR, MICHAEL KEENAN & FREDDY BASANTES JR.
MILLBURY, MASSACHUSETTS

In a perfect world, there would be no bullies at all. That goes without saying. Ideally, there would be no reason for any child to be afraid to go to school to learn, or to play with other kids, or to try new things. We can all hope for and work towards that goal, and it's the impetus behind no-tolerance bullying policies that are springing up all over the country. These state that both parties in a bullying situation are punished with suspension if it escalates to a physical level, regardless of who instigated the altercation.

Unfortunately, these rules can be counter-productive, despite the good intentions behind them. They're simply not enough to curb bullying and they can make a child who is already a victim feel even more powerless and helpless than before.

Freddy's son is 14 and suffered from bullying when he transitioned to a new school. One of the kids kept pushing him around, touching his belongings, and calling him names. He did everything he thought he was supposed to do—asked the kid to stop, told the teacher, and removed himself to a quiet space to calm down—but unfortunately, none of these things were enough to stop the taunting and the violations of personal space.

Eventually, the boy had no choice but to shove back.

Thankfully, the principal deviated from that no-tolerance policy in favor of evaluating all the evidence to make sure that true justice prevailed. She decided that Freddy's son took all the right steps to deescalate the situation before resorting to physical defense. He was not punished.

(The best part of the story comes after the incident, when the bully returned to school and asked Freddy's son, "Hey, we're cool, right?" Now, they get along fine.)

Anyone who believes that bullying isn't an issue with kids today is probably close to a child who isn't telling the whole truth about his or her experiences at school. The kids who are honest make the truth clear: it's a day-to-day part of a child's life, and despite common opinion, it's a much bigger problem than it used to be.

Why? Kids feel like they can't fight back. They're trained to be submissive to bullies. They're trained to ignore it, to let it go, to be the "bigger person." They're trained to be walking targets, because we all know that bullies are attracted to the kids who won't defend themselves. No-tolerance rules just exacerbate this issue much of the time. Good kids don't want to be kicked out of school, no matter the reason, so they are taught to stand idle while they are being bullied.

They submit themselves to abuse so they don't have to submit themselves to suspension.

Further, they're taught to keep bullying to themselves. What if they decide to tell an adult who doesn't believe them? What if the bully turns around and lies about what happened? Will they be accused of being the guilty party? Will they lose that argument and be suspended instead? Will their "tattling" result in even more bullying?

You can see why submission and silence may seem like the best option.

We work with kids on a daily basis at Life Skill Martial Arts in Millbury, Massachusetts. Many of them come to us, at some point or another, with hard questions about bullying. They've done everything they were taught to do—tell their teachers, their parents, and their principal—and very little, if anything, has actually happened to make the abuse stop. Every adult party has spoken to one another and agreed that something must be done, but none of them have actually moved to resolve the issue on behalf of the child.

So what happens when adults say, "Don't worry, we'll take care of it," and then they don't?

The child can keep making attempts to diffuse tense situations, of course. They can try standing tall, making eye contact, using a strong voice, keeping their distance, and putting their hands up in a firm "stop" signal. These are all important skills to try first, but if the bully continues to violate their space, and especially if the bully makes a move to strike... it's time to block, hit back, create space as quickly and efficiently as possible, and use that space to extract themselves from the situation and immediately find an adult who can take control.

If a bully makes it clear that violence is his goal, children must stand up and defend themselves to show the bully that the behavior cannot—will not—continue.

We find that parents are generally in support of these measures. When we discuss this in our classes with parents present, they often applaud, nod, or find their child in the classroom and make firm eye contact, which promises they will be on their child's side in any conflict where everything was done to deescalate and avoid violence.. Many of them know it's their own responsibility to teach their kids to be able to stand up for themselves.

We're honored to assist them in doing that for their children. We enjoy teaching Kung Fu and other styles of martial arts, but we are aware that self-defense is only part of the toolkit that children must be given in order to cope effectively with tense interactions with those who don't have their best interests at heart. Nothing is more off-putting to a bully than confidence, so empowerment is the critical foundation needed for any person—young or old—to become bully-proof.

Some people may wonder how teaching someone to punch targets and break boards and develop katas and forms help little Johnny go from the shy kid who's not willing to stand up for himself to the kid who's ready to look someone in the eye and defend himself.

It's harder than it seems. Building confidence has to come first, and that requires discipline and consistency over long periods of time. Children need to develop their physique so they can feel in control of their bodies and their space and their movements. They need to become confident in their voices. They need to feel comfortable making eye contact. Thankfully, these confidence-building skills are already embedded in martial arts. Strong bodies, strong movements, strong voices, strong eye contact, and strong gestures become natural habits in the way martial arts students interact with the world around them.

It helps to ditch the militaristic attitude and teach in ways that kids will enjoy. They want to see everything as an interesting activity, and they crave positivity, so we teach them that confidence in themselves is a good way to make their parents and grandparents happy, to do better in school, and to make friends. They learn that their lives will be more fun and rewarding if they can learn to interact with people in a strong, confident manner.

At the same time, martial arts demands that they train physically. Our students push themselves a little past what they used to believe their limits were; they challenge themselves, and we challenge them, and they enjoy seeing what they're really capable of when they dedicate themselves to improving over time. They learn that success is all about setting goals, making plans to achieve them, and then sticking to that plan until the end. Doing so gives them a consistent routine, which helps build confidence in their ability to accomplish anything they set their minds to.

They sweat and have fun and gain confidence in their physical ability at the same time. At the end of each class, we like to remind them what they accomplished the week before, and show them how much better they've grown just since then: "Last week you could only kick this high, and now look at you. You're kicking over your head!" Building their self-esteem goes hand-in-hand with building their confidence. They grow to love the practice of putting in hard work to achieve results they can be proud of.

Of course this confidence translates to other areas of their lives. It shows when they present heir projects in school, when they speak their minds, when they're showing off their skills, when they're given opportunities to lead, and when they're expressing themselves freely. As they become more confident in their bodies and abilities, they're willing to try more difficult things, which builds even more confidence.

It is a slow process to use martial arts to develop the life skills they need to become bully-proof, but it's a natural process that is time-tested and true.

However, in the words of Mike Tyson, "Everyone has a plan until they're punched in the face." Our self-assurance has a nasty habit of completely disappearing whenever someone puts their hands on us; it doesn't matter how good a person is at their forms, voice, posture, or physical abilities. As soon as they're in a high-stakes situation, many people forget everything they've learned and return to their previous state of fear and panic. so confidence is only half of what a child needs. The self-defense skills must be taught and reinforced, until they come automatically in a tense situation. It's very important in training to teach kids how to become comfortable with getting pushed and getting hit so they don't fall apart and forget all their training if it happens outside of the classroom.

We also see the effectiveness in bringing students to the front of the class to let them demonstrate activities in front of other kids. This rewards them for their dedication and gives them the opportunity to practice these critical skills under pressure.

If your child is being bullied at school, please consider a good martial-arts program designed for kids to help them develop the confidence and self-defense skills they need. Naturally, sports are a good way to build bodily control and strength, but with sports comes competition, which can sometimes make kids even more cruel to one another. This attitude is, unfortunately, egged on by many coaches and parents at games.

Martial arts really is an exceptional method of incorporating a whole scope of lessons a child needs to move forward confidently in the world. No other activity or hobby focuses so equally on the mind and body, on long-term goals and short-term goals alike, and on improving not just your performance on the floor, but in your whole life. It's not about winning against someone else. It's about being better than you were yesterday, and being confident in that progress.

Stan Tabor began training in martial arts in 1972. He is the owner of Life Skill Martial Arts. He started studying martial arts and western boxing at age 12. Began to practice Mantis Kung Fu in 1975 and was certified to teach in 1986. He studied martial arts in China for many years as the disciple of Grandmaster Liu Chengde in Jinan City, Shandong Province.

Since 1989, Mr. Tabor has been instructing students in traditional martial arts and reality based self-defense on his 4 acre training center in Millbury Massachusetts.

For more information, visit www.lifeskillmartialarts.com.

Freddy Basantes Jr. has held many jobs from electronics field service to warehouse work. He then strated working in the medical field, delivering and setting up medical equipment in clients' homes. After that, he started working as a CAN in a transitional care unit in a hospital helping patiends recover so they can either go home or into a long-term care facility.

He has finally found his passion in helping families through martial arts and hasn't looked back since.

Michael Keenan is an instructor at Life Skill Martial Arts. He has been practicing martial arts for 17 years. He has also worked as a math teacher in both private and public schools.

CHAPTER 2: PEACE THROUGH DEFENSE

BY KENNETH MACKENZIE
ATCO, NEW JERSEY

My family moved more often than the average family, so I dealt with bullying more than the average kid. My father changed jobs a lot, and by the time I finished my elementary years, I'd attended seven different schools in Indiana, Michigan, and New Jersey.

Children are curious about newcomers just like adults are. Whenever I walked into a new school, I could feel the weight of all the questions my new classmates were asking themselves and each other during those first few days: "Is he tough? Is he a wuss?

Can he fight? Is he a victim? Is he going to run the schoolyard, or is he going to be quiet and submissive?"

This was a different age, before the strict no-tolerance rules that many school systems have in place today. Playground fights were still a daily event, and I found myself dragged into a lot of them. The playground monitor would stand nearby when a fight broke out to make sure it didn't get out-of-hand, and if it did, they'd drag us apart and tell us to go to opposite sides of the playground. Nobody got in trouble.

I will never forget my father's words: "You better get out there, and you got to fight. You have to prove that you're willing to defend yourself. If not, you're going to be a victim your entire life." So that's what I did.

An old schoolmate of mine I hadn't seen for 30 years recently respond to an ad I put out about my bully-defense seminar with the words, "Ken, weren't you a bully?"

Those words hit me. Hard. They forced me to evaluate the memories I had of my childhood and after awhile, I realized he was right. I'd been victimized so much in my early days that I wanted payback. In high school, when I'd physically gotten bigger and my martial-arts skills were more developed, I saw no wrong in trying them out on the same kids who had picked on me as a child.
I became a bully.

Later, I was at a restaurant and saw, a few tables away, the face of a man who kicked and teased me when I was a child. He was a little older, sure, and a little grayer, but it was definitely the same guy who assaulted me on the very first day of school in New Jersey, and who had given me a degrading nickname that stuck with me for years.

He noticed me, but said nothing, so I called his name: "Bruce?"

"Ken?" he said.

"Yeah," I said. "It's great to see you.

We got into a little conversation. He seemed a bit timid. He'd apparently never put two and two together to realize that I targeted him because of the level of torment he'd inflicted on me first. Both of us were gracious about it. We had a couple of laughs, shook hands, and apologized. At the end, we gave each other a hug. I remember leaving the restaurant that day feeling just a little bit better.

Now, when I encounter old classmates, I make it a point to address the elephant in the room: "I'm sorry if I was not always the nicest guy back in school, but I remember that you were the bully until I got bigger and stronger and returned the favor. None of it was right, so let's shake hands with a new understanding."

This has given me even more drive to help my community be a better place than it was when I left it as a child. I started in judo when I was in preschool, and Hapkido and Taekwondo in the mid seventies. I opened MacKenzie's Martial Arts in New Jersey in 1983 with an offering that was relatively innovative at the time—a program specifically for kids. I've made it my mission to grow not just strong kids, but positive ones, who are doing the right thing in life, staying out of trouble, and being a friend to others. At this point in my life, I have seen over ten thousand children come and go.

Because I have been the bullied *and* the bully, I know both sides of the psychological game very well. Yes, I turned out okay, along with many others my age who were bullied during our childhoods. So why the sudden jump in kids who are seriously struggling with what we survived with relative ease?

Bullies have grown more sophisticated than ever to accommodate new rules limiting their usual, simple behaviors. In the sixties and seventies, two kids had an explosion on the playground, and that was it. Even if you lost the fight, you proved yourself to be tough if you were willing to swing back.

Today, kids are not allowed to defend themselves. If they are physically assaulted, they are expected to stand there, take the beating, and *then* go tell somebody. This is a very confusing societal expectation to me, as both a martial arts instructor and a parent who believes that it is our human right to defend ourselves. Pacifism is all well and good, but children who are taught not to defend themselves quickly lose confidence and self-esteem and wonder why adults don't feel as though they are worth protecting. Meanwhile, the bullies are getting stronger and smarter. All of this creates a recipe for a nationwide bullying crisis.

Some people out there think that bullying isn't that big of a problem, but the data suggests otherwise. There are 74 million children 18 and under in the United States, and over 20% of those kids have reported being bullied at least weekly, if not daily. Those are just the children who aren't too embarrassed or ashamed to admit it; we can assume the real number is much higher.

Bullies search for easy targets and hold onto them as long as they can. When kids are trained to not fight back, they can become victims for years. They learn to hang their hands low and look down at their shoes, and exhibit all the behaviors of a person who isn't willing to defend themselves. Their physiology becomes a self-fulfilling prophecy.

Ideally, that child would be moved to a new school for a fresh start and a clean slate, but that's not in the cards for most families. So what happens to a child, emotionally and psychologically, when they're abused by others for years with no justice? They're either going to grow up looking for payback like I did, a phenomenon that only creates more bullies, or they will descend into such a dark place of low confidence that they may never find their way out.

We've had a number of suicides in South Jersey within a couple of miles of my school, and I always wonder what would've happened if that child had been in my school, if I could have partnered with their parents to help. What if that child heard, just once, "It doesn't matter what the other person is saying. No one determines the value that you have, just by being you." Helping kids that way is a long process, and a slow process, and a difficult process, but the investment is worth it when you consider the consequences of not doing it.

Every child has greatness inside of them. Every child has the potential to grow up to be the best car mechanic, the most talented builder, the bravest soldier, the smartest business man, the kindest teacher, or whatever their dream may be. But it takes confidence to get there, and if a child believes what a bully says—that they're no good, worthless, and weak—they may never take the chances they need to take to get where they deserve to be. That may be one of the most tragic results of bullying.

I've been fortunate to work with Grandmaster Ji Han Jae in the Washington, D.C. area, who wears a patch that says "Might Before Right." It means, "Become mighty and powerful, but for all of the right reasons." His other favorite saying is, "Peace through defense knowledge."

I never get into fights in real life. I tell my students, "I'm a big guy with a lot of fighting experience. If I wanted to beat someone up, it would be easy. But I would much rather make friends." Being strong and trained gives me the confidence I need to be outgoing. I don't feel threatened by most people, and I feel comfortable going up to perfect strangers and families to tell them about what I do. I can look people in the eye and smile without fear. I've learned not to put my chest out in arrogance, but to walk tall knowing who I am, what I am, and where I'm going.

People who can stand that way give off a positive vibe that helps bullyproof them. If we can get kids to start feeling better about who they are and what skills they have, their classmates will naturally treat them with more respect.

I use an animal analogy with my students to convey this important point. I ask them to imagine a squirrel trapped in a pillowcase or a sack. Not even the toughest kid out there would put his hand inside, right? Why?

"Because that squirrel would tear your hand off!" they tell me.

Even children know that the smallest, most helpless creature will fight back with everything it has when it is presented with no other option. It doesn't matter how big someone is. With the right spirit, and good confidence that you can defend yourself if need be, bullies will sense that you aren't someone they need to engage with in a negative manner.

Any activity that builds a kid's confidence and helps them identify a strong part of their identity is a good thing, whether it's a sport, a game like chess, art, or martial arts. The other part of the equation, of course, is making sure every child has strong allies.

My children are adults, now. I have one son, and two daughters who are all adults. They're amazing kids. Two of them enduring bullying as children.

Your first reaction as a parent, when your child breaks the news to you that they are being bullied, will be indignation and disgust. How dare anyone victimize your child! But what's more important than your emotions is your ability to communicate with your child. Of all the students I've seen come in and out of the doors of my schools, the ones who are comfortable enough to talk to their parents well and often are always the most successful in navigating hard situations.

One of the biggest mistakes parents can make is making themselves unavailable for conversation at any point in a child's development. At a young age, children talk a lot about things that are frivolous and pointless. It can be tempting when a parent is busy or stressed to put them off, to give them half-hearted answers that make it clear where their attention is (and isn't), or to ignore them outright.

Boom... suddenly, they're in middle school, and they're not communicating, and they're moody, and they're keeping secrets. That's when parents suddenly get on that "I need to start talking to my kid!" train. Is it too late to build communication and trust?

To those parents, I encourage you to be human. It's okay to sit down with your child with no media, no email, no texting, no phone calls, and say, "Let's get together and talk." Tell them you've made some mistakes. Tell them you want to do better, and tell them you're open to suggestions on how to do that. Tell them you want to talk more. Tell them you're sorry

Trust requires a certain vulnerability that a child of that age, especially one experiencing bullying, may not be willing to give. If you give it first, it will help them let their guard down and open up. Children instinctually want a good relationship with their parents. If the relationship has gone sideways, creating some communication barriers, those can be brought down with a little bit of old-fashioned love, and honesty in your mistakes is always a great place to start.

Another mistake many parents make is to present oversimplified, unhelpful solutions like, "Just ignore it," or "don't listen to them," or "walk away." If that's the best advice you can offer a child and it doesn't work, where can they turn? Who can they go to when the person who cares for them most gave them their best response, and it did nothing? They will feel as though they have nowhere else to go for answers.

We are given two ears and only one mouth, so we should listen more than we speak. Listening to a child and letting them know that you see their problems and acknowledge their complexity is a good first step. Keep that door of communication open, so the child knows they have an ally who will keep helping them come up with new solutions when the old ones fail.

Teachers play another key role in creating bully-proof children. So many teachers want their kids to do well and be safe, but they are constrained by the rules of their administration, and can't necessarily protect their students they way they wish they could. How can they help without stepping out of line?

In my classroom, we do what I call mat-chats. We sit in a circle and go around, giving each child a chance to speak their mind and share their ideas. The kid that's been bullied is probably the last one that's going to stand up and speak, and that's okay. If they're not ready, I say, "We'll come back to you."

It's critical to create a classroom culture where bullying is not vogue and empathy is fashionable. That requires input from everybody, and it's best to start very, very early. Many teachers emphasize conflict resolution in the 4th and 5th grade, but at some point, attention is shifted away from it, and those concepts become ignored.

For a teacher, dealing with a bullying situation is nerve-wracking enough without the cheering-mob effect, so separating the bully and the bullied from the group is important. It's human nature to want some action, but the clamoring crowd only exacerbates a bullying scenario. Afford the two parties the opportunity to speak to one another with just the teacher there are moderator.

When I was a child, I got into an accident where my leg was impaired, and suffered several knee and hip surgeries and years of being unable to walk well as a result. The kids called me Limpy, and I can still hear them laughing whenever they'd kick their legs out to make me trip and drop my books or fall. Martial arts saved my life, because my training gave me the physical, mental, and emotional strength to channel that negative energy into a passion for helping children overcome their difficulties.

When I see a child looking uncertainly at their surroundings or depressed, I can identify that there's something going on they're not ready to talk about, yet. As a teacher, I simply cannot force them to communicate before they're comfortable doing so, but what I can do is say all the things I wish I'd heard from teachers as a child: "Hey, you're doing great, champ. I'm glad you're here. It's always a better day when I have you in my class. Thanks for being awesome."

If a parent came to me with a kid that has a bullying problem, I would likely recommend that they sign up for a child's martial arts program like mine. I have a disproportionally high number of single moms bringing their children to my school, looking for a positive role model and a teammate in helping strengthen their child's confidence. Introducing your child to a new peer group introduced in a controlled atmosphere, like Cub Scouts, is also a good idea. Making friends is making allies and having allies is building confidence. That's something that can really help a child of any age.

When kids come to me with problems, I almost always respond with, "How about you go home and, when you're ready, tell your mom what you just told me? She's the most important person in your whole life, and you should let her know about that sort of thing." As a third party, it's easier for me to ask certain questions than it would be for parents to ask them, and my words sometimes have a different effect.

Babies don't come with instructional manuals, and raising them is one giant high-stakes experiment where the variables are always changing. Another helping hand never hurts. Please don't hesitate to contact me with questions or for more information about my program, or even just to chat.

Ken MacKenzie's martial arts journey began in 1968 at a YMCA just outside of Indianapolis, Indiana. The style was "Judo", and this early experience was to lead him to both a lifetime pursuit of martial arts excellence and adventure.

As a child, MacKenzie's family moved a lot. In fact, he attended seven elementary schools before his elementary school tenure concluded. As a result, he often found himself within the sights of schoolyard and neighborhood bullies. Fighting, win or lose, was commonplace for this young man. Dealing with bullies was not MacKenzie's only challenge. As a child, he dealt with a number of major illnesses and injuries. Following a series of hip and knee surgeries, and in an effort to rehab his legs, MacKenzie started his career in "Korean Karate" (aka. 'TaeKwon-Do' and 'Hapkido') in the mid 1970's…a career that has now spanned some five decades.

MacKenzie's TaeKwon-Do and Hapkido training was hard, and it took him over seven years to achieve the coveted rank of Blackbelt. During that time, he learned much more than merely kicks and punches. The traditional martial arts education on which he had embarked had developed in him a strong sense of self-worth and confidence. He had also learned that his strongest tool for self-defense was in fact his mind. To this day, and in addition to being very strong physically, MacKenzie is known as both a "martial arts intellect" and a "warrior of virtue".

While studying Law & Justice in college, MacKenzie opened his first martial arts school. Even before the release of the iconic "Karate Kid" movie, MacKenzie's Martial Arts was to become the first all-children's professional martial arts school in the nation.

Having won over two-hundred local, state, regional and national martial arts tournaments, MacKenzie went on to win three (3) world championships in South Korea. Still going strong, MacKenzie is the owner of several professional martial arts schools (aka. "dojangs") in southern New Jersey, and is the president of the "World SinMoo Hapkido Federation" under 'DoJuNim' Ji, Han Jae, the founder of Korean Hapkido. In 2010, MacKenzie became the first American-born to achieve the rank of 10th Degree Blackbelt in Korean Hapkido, and is the heir-apparent as per the founder. MacKenzie has been featured on the cover of five popular martial arts magazines, and has been seen and heard on both radio and television worldwide. A 'Hall-of-Famer', MacKenzie was named by TaeKwon-Do Times Magazine as the "International Grandmaster of the Year".

With all of his achievements, 'Grandmaster' Kenneth MacKenzie is clear when he tells people that his greatest achievements surround the work that he does in the interest of youth.

For more information, visit www.mackenziesmartialarts.com, or call (856) 346-1111..

CHAPTER 3: LEARNING TO ADD WITH BLACK BELT MATH

BY SHARON RUECKERT
GLENDALE, ARIZONA

My husband and I have two martial-arts schools in the Phoenix, Arizona area. Jessiah is a sixth-degree black belt, and I'm a third-degree; between the two of us, we have almost forty years of martial-arts experience. We see bullying two or three times a month. My students will share it with me, parents will share it with me, and sometimes I see it out in the community.

When parents sign their child up for martial arts training it always comes down to 4 reasons, fitness, self-esteem, discipline or self-defense. Almost every time a parent chooses self-defense as the primary reason for signing their child up it is bullying related. When I look at the parents face as they tell me about what happened or is happening to their child at school with bullying I see pain, frustration and worry. I can't help but ask, what do they know about bullying, what have they taught their child to do about it and how are they going to prevent it from happening in the future. These questions usually bring a look of defeat on their face. I hear a variety of answers, like "I tell my child who is being bullied to, just walk away."

Maybe the first time, but it is not a permanent solution. That's not a coping skill; it's a sign that a person has absolutely no other tools in their toolbox to handle a situation. When you give up on conversation and on protecting yourself, you've given up on resolving the conflict in a healthy way.

It also sets a precedent for giving up in the face of difficulty moving forward. That child is going to continue to walk away from things that feel confrontational. That child is going to grow up and walk away from jobs, relationships, and opportunities because they were taught that running from hard circumstances is better than perseverance and resolution.

Instead of making them feel helpless, children should instead be taught and trained with the proper coping skills so they feel confident and informed: squaring their shoulders and facing problems head-on.

First let's get on the same page as the school districts by defining Bullying. What is bullying? Olweus is by far the most popular bully prevention program used in schools. This organization defines bullying as "an aggressive behavior that is intentional and involves an imbalance of power. Most often, it is repeated over time." By working backwards with this definition we can see "**overtime**" sounds like a habit. "**Imbalance of Power**" meaning we must give children their power back, and knowledge is power. And finally, it must be "**Intentional**" so we have to provide a measuring tool for our children to understand the other persons "intent."

Understanding the Power of Habits.

Parents are children's first teachers. Parents teach their children to brush their teeth, have manners, do their homework, say thank you ("Johnny what do we say?") These are all habits. So it would stand to reason that if parents can teach these habits they can create and teach their children habits that will prevent bullying. Habits are a result of a process called chunking. Chunking is where the brain converts a sequence of actions into an automatic routine. Some are simple like brushing your teeth, some are complex like driving (when is the last time you stressed out about backing your car out of the garage? You don't, it's a habit)

A study was done at Duke University that estimated habits rather than conscious decision making, shape 45% of the choices we make every day. With that high of a percentage shouldn't we know how habits are formed?

There is a process in our brain that creates habits. A three-step loop. The Cue, Routine and Reward. **Cue** is the trigger that tells the brain to go into auto pilot – to use the chunk/ or loop. **Routine** could be physical, mental or emotional. The **Reward** helps the brain figure out if this loop is worth remembering for the future. Over time this loop/habit becomes more and more automatic. The **Cue** and **Reward** becomes neurologically intertwined until a sense of craving emerges. Once a habit/loop is established the brain stops fully participating in the decision making, things go on auto pilot.

Bullying becomes a habit for some people, a form of communication. The reward is getting what they want from the situation, whether it is attention, an object or simply their way. Being a victim of bullying can become a habit too. If your child continues to be bullied without any additional coping skills their loop of being the one bullied is reinforced and eventually their behavior goes on auto pilot. They become adults and continue to find themselves in bad relationships, situations and experiences.

Knowledge is Power:

There are 4 different kinds of bullying. Physical, verbal, cyber and friend exclusion.

Physical bullying is when someone is hit by an object, punching, throwing, kicking. This is usually the type of bullying that gets reported because the aftermath can be seen via bruises, broken things, or ripped clothing. But this is usually not the first time the bully has "bullied" the victim. It is just the first time it was caught by teachers. SO when parents tell me the bullying has been going on for months but the teacher/school did nothing, it is usually because bullying finally went physical and the teachers/ school finally had the proof to get involved.

The other three types of bullying are harder to identify and to stop at the school level. **Verbal bullying** is when the bully starts berating the victim. Calling them names, defaming their character, laughing at them, mocking them. When I point out how many times we as adults display this very behavior in our personal lives the parents are shocked. How many times have you yelled at someone in traffic (road rage) said some politician was stupid, or cursed in front of your child? What they see is what they will accept as normal. SO if they see you do it to others, wouldn't it be logical to assume that they think it is ok for someone else to do it to them?

Cyber bullying is a relatively new strand of bullying. It involves anything that could go online. With all the social media streams it is almost the norm. If you go online to any social media site you can find an example of cyber bullying within a few minutes. Children are gaining access to the internet at a young age. I see 3 year old children with a tablet (usually their own) all the time. I can't count the times I see parents give their smart phone to a very young child to "entertain them" so the parent can talk with me. When I see this I usually ask the parent if they have an online policy for their children established at home. The answer is usually "we will do this when they get older"

Unfortunately, if you give your child an electronic device that can go online than that is when you must have an online policy established. Regardless of the child's age. Go online with your child, and talk about good and bad behavior, and what is expected in your family. Limit their time and access. Don't make their cyber time a reward. I see parents all the time negotiate online time as the reward.

Don't be so engrossed in your own phone or tablets in front of your child. When they are at an activity, put your phone away and watch, be present. Don't talk on the phone in your car, or at the grocery store when your children are with you. It can wait. Show your children an example of being present in their lives. Many parents when I first say this will argue with me about how they "go" everywhere with their child, they are present. Being physically present is very different from being emotionally present.

The final type of bullying is **friend exclusion.** This is when the bully deliberately isolates a person or excludes them from group activities. We all want to be accepted and belong and when we exclude someone it affects their self-esteem.

Defining Intent:

I have an easy way to teach even the youngest children to identify the intent of an action or a behavior before calling someone a bully. We do this by offering a skill called black-belt math.
Black belts like to add friends, not subtract friends. So we've got to learn how to A.D.D. in a situation that could escalate into full-blown bullying. **Ask, direct, decide.**

First, we're going to *ask* the child to quit the offensive behavior.

"Could you not put your hands on me?"
"Could you not talk to me like that?"
"Can you stop saying those hurtful things so we can talk this through?"

Then we're going to *direct* them to do something that will deescalate the situation.

"If you want to talk to me, please stand a little bit further away from me, because having you in my space makes me feel uncomfortable."

"Instead of calling me names, tell me why you're treating me like this."

"I've been standing in line like I'm supposed to. Go to the back of the line so we don't have a problem."

Then we're going to let them ***decide*** whether they want to be a friend or a bully.

I've been teaching this for well over a decade, and it's become my signature lesson for students of all ages who come through my programs. The minute somebody comes up to my husband and I and tells us about bullying, whether it's a parent or a child, I'll say, "Did you use black-belt math?"

With this tool, a child knows that they have something grounded to bring into a chaotic equation the instant someone bullies them. This also creates empathy, because instead of having two kids fighting over control, it's one child offering the other child the opportunity to make the right choices, and empowering both parties to solve the problem together.

I've heard kids all the time say, "I used black-belt math, Mrs. Rueckert, and I found out that this person just didn't have any friends and didn't know how to talk to people. Now I sit at lunch with them and hang out with them all the time!"

I've taught this skill to preschoolers and married couples, and every age in-between. In addition to my young students, I also have several teachers—elementary and high-school—and two principals who are my students and have freely used my black-belt math during the school year, though they may alter the name to suit their school, such as *cougar math* or *warrior math*. Whatever you call it, this process of asking, directing, and deciding empowers children and adults to take back control while still being empathetic and giving the bully the opportunity to pause and evaluate his or her behavior.

It also allows children to learn the difference between being bullied and being sensitive, because kids who live in households where parents shelter them from every bump and bruise often have a hard time understanding the difference. As we know, bullying is purposeful and persistent, and anything less than that is probably a miscommunication that is far more easily resolved.

Once a child understands the intent of an action or an offensive statement they now are able to deal with it through appropriate communication.

Now we know how bullying is defined in the school districts, we have learned about forming Habits, and understand how to define Intent with Black Belt math, what do we do with the information? We communicate. We don't fix the problem right away!

It's counterintuitive for a parent, I know, but the minute you rush in to fix your child's problem or run to their defense, you've robbed them of an opportunity to learn to resolve an issue themselves.

However, when a bullying situation occurs, one of the most important lines of communication is the one between parent and child, so be present. Ask questions about what happened, and then ask *more* questions if you need to. Write their answers down. This shows the child that—though you will not do all the work for them—they are not facing the challenge alone. They deserve the opportunity to solve their own problems, but they deserve to know they have someone on their side.

Kids don't have decades of experience to measure things by, so they are constantly building and growing new perceptions on the fly for most things they come across. For example, children who are given video games in lieu of strong communication may learn that hurting or even killing something is the way to win in this world. Without a strong adult to guide that perception—"Remember, it's just a game. Don't get lost in it. It's fake."—things like that can take hold before you know it.

We need to teach empathy first. We need to teach children to think rationally, not rashly.

Tell Not Tattle:

Telling is informing, tattling is trying to get someone else in trouble.

I always teach my kids at an early, early age to start by telling me the who, what, when, where of an encounter with a bully. This teaches them the difference between telling and tattling. Then comes the *why*.

Maybe someone pushes a kid out of the lunch line and takes his spot. Once I get the who, what, when, and where, I would ask, "*Why* do you think he did that?"

Let's say the child responds with, "I think he did it because he was hungry."

Now that we have a grounded place to start, I can start asking the big questions to guide the child's perception of what happened. "Do you think that you should be mad at him because he was hungry and he felt he needed to be first? Did you tell him you weren't happy with him pushing you? Why do you think he was so hungry today? Did something happen in class that made him grumpy? Was he in a hurry to finish his lunch and be somewhere else? If he had asked you politely, would you have let him take your spot? Have you and he had problems in the lunchroom before that would make him feel as though he couldn't be polite with you?"

Bullying and victimization both happen when children feel like they don't have control of a situation. It's natural for children to react emotionally to situations that are out of their control, or situations they don't understand. When their thoughts are guided with facts and empathy, they can start to look at situations more like scientists, and then like people who can reach out instead of lash out.

I think that's the most important thing that we must teach children in today's society is great communication skills. There is no reason why a toddler should be learning formative skills from an iPad and not from an adult looking them in the face and giving them their undivided attention. How else will they learn body language? Facial expressions? Conversation? How will they learn to express their preferences and discomforts to those around them without becoming overly emotional and attention-seeking?

Communication is a huge part of martial arts, and something students learn naturally just by being in class. When an instructor speaks, the children are expected to verbally respond in a strong voice, either by affirming that they've heard the direction or by answering the question. Both of these serve as confirmation that everyone is paying attention to the right things.

The good news? You don't need martial arts to practice this. When you speak, expect your children to answer, and then *return that courtesy*. When your child speaks to you, put your phone down. Put your book on the table. Look them in the eye. Consider their words and consider your response. If you're in a situation where you cannot give them the attention they deserve, ask them if the conversation can wait, and then offer a legitimate alternative: "Can this wait until I make this phone call? Can this wait until we finish lunch? Can this wait until after I go to the bathroom? Can this wait until tonight?" Consider that agreement a promise.

This teaches children two things: 1) that they are deserving of your undivided attention, and 2) that the way to handle any problem is to stop, breathe, and then be present, patient, empathetic, and understanding.

Children do what we do, so we need to be actively exhibiting behaviors that send a strong message: "See what I'm doing? *This* is what's expected of you. *This* is what's allowed. *This* is what good behavior means. *These* are the habits you should form as you grow so you can be respected and respectful as an adult."

If we start doing that as a society then we're going to have a lot less problems with bullying.

If you're interested in hearing more about our thoughts on bullying, children, and black-belt math, get in touch with us on our website, inspirationmartialarts.com. I look forward to hearing from you.

Sharon Rueckert has been working with children over 20 years. She has worked in several fortune 500 companies in both Human Resources and Customer relations before opening her on business teaching Martial Arts. Sharon is very active in her community both professionally and personally. She is a 3rd degree black belt Certified Instructor with the American Taekwondo Association. She owns 2 schools in the Phoenix, AZ area.

For more information, visit www.inspirationmartialarts.com.

CHAPTER 4:
IT TAKES A VILLAGE...
TO END BULLYING

BY KIMBERLY TANNY
AURORA, COLORADO

We know that every child is unique and deserving of the tools he or she needs to resist the urge to bully others, and to stand up for themselves if the need arises. Empowering kids as individuals is imperative to keeping them emotionally and physically safe in a society where bullying is still a huge problem.

However, I believe it takes the combined effort of everyone in the community to make strong, respectful leaders of our children. Our culture generally prefers to ignore and deny the bullying epidemic, but if you're reading this, I'm assuming you have acknowledged the existence of bullying in our world. The next step is to get *everyone* involved in conquering it, because kids, teachers, and parents can't do it alone.

When I was a child, I used to feel so powerless against the kids who would pull the chair out from under me, or say mean things to my face and behind my back. I'm going to guess that feeling of helplessness in bullied children hasn't changed over the years. For anyone to expect kids to "just work it out" on their own is unfair, infeasible, and irresponsible. Who can they count on for help?

Teachers are on the front lines in the fight against bullying. They spend an average of 650 to 800 hours or more a year with their students, and many children spend more time with their teachers than with their parents. They do have a responsibility to enforce good behavior, but their *primary* role is to educate. They have the power to teach values, but that power is limited. Just like the children, the teachers cannot pull the weight of bully-proofing the community on their own.

Parents, of course, must realize that they carry the bulk of the responsibility to teach values and moral aptitude in the home, so children will take those traits out into their community and demonstrate them in public for other kids to see. However, in a world where single parents are becoming more and more common, parents also need a little bit of help from other members of the community to make sure the good behaviors they expect inside of the house are enforced outside of it as well.

So eliminating bullying requires the involvement of the children, the parents, the teachers, the administrators, and other community members like martial arts instructors, sports coaches, and any other adult with an influence in the life of a child. Kids learn by example, and if the adults they admire exemplify anti-bullying behaviors and teach anti-bullying values, that child will more than likely follow in their footsteps. There must not be any inconsistencies in the way those values are instilled and enforced across the board.

One solution to bullying that has been proven ineffective is mediating, where an adult serves as a third party in helping kids discuss and resolve their conflicts. There are so many problems with this strategy, first of which is the assumption that the bullied child will feel comfortable coming forward in the first place. Other kids and adults alike have spent the last few years hammering the "don't be a snitch or a tattle-tale" idea, and in the next breath we tell them, "If something happens, tell an adult." Imagine how confused the average child must feel. Which problems should they bring forward, and which ones should they keep to themselves?

Additionally, kids who are bullied are often victimized and targeted over a long period of time, so imagine how uncomfortable and terrifying it would be to sit face-to-face with someone you'll have to see every day for the rest of the year, someone who will probably continue making your life miserable just for speaking up.

What's more, many victims are often told by bullies, "You better not tell anyone." So the odds of them telling the mediator the entire story while sitting across from someone who is likely to deny the whole thing are pretty slim.

Zero-tolerance policies are also hugely ineffective, in my opinion. Threatening all children with suspension and detention and punishment if they play any role in a bullying scenario is so counterproductive. Imagine all of the negative reactions they may have to being sent away from the resources they need to improve and learn. They are *children*, and they need to be taught to correct their behavior via appropriate consequences and reinforcement of good values. We must resist the urge to exile or demonize them, because bullies are as precious as the kids they victimize.

Bullying victims, on the other hand, shouldn't be ignored or coddled. Instead, they should be empowered with the knowledge and opportunities they need to stand up for themselves. This will reinforce with bullies that their behavior will not stand, and it will increase the victims' confidence as well.

I've been training in martial arts for 16 years, and I own the Tanny Academy of Martial Arts in Aurora, Colorado. I have taught martial arts internationally, and one of my specialties is working with children, parents, and even school teachers (when I can) to make our kids and our community bully-proof.

Martial arts has never been just about learning the kicks and breaking boards. There is a huge focus on what we call the tenets of Taekwondo: courtesy, integrity, perseverance, self-control, and indomitable spirit.

Courtesy, of course, goes hand-in-hand with respect, which is the foundation on which successful martial arts study is built. In our school, we enforce behaviors like saying ma'am and sir and please and thank you. We bow at appropriate times, and we do not interrupt the figures of authority or even other students. I firmly believe that a child who respects others is less likely to be a bully.

Integrity is doing the right thing even if nobody is watching. A child who understands this concept will be positive and respectful to their peers whether adults are present or not. That positivity goes a long way in helping kids police themselves and one another, which is empowering for everyone.

The third tenet of Taekwondo is perseverance. Of course, in martial arts, we start the beginners on front kicks, then side kicks, and then advance from there. We'd never try to teach a child to do a flying side kick on their first day. Even when taking baby steps, there will be times when even the best student won't be able to perform certain techniques right away. Perseverance is awareness that no one succeeds at something if they give up on it. Temporary failure is okay. It teaches us and helps us become stronger and stronger until we achieve what we set out to do.

The fourth tenet is self-control—not just of your body, but of your mind as well. You can see why this is an important tool in a child's arsenal against bullying. Being able to keep yourself from lashing out at others in your worst moments is a skill that many adults don't have, let alone children. Everyone could stand to work on that, and emphasizing it with kids is an excellent way to teach them how to keep their cool in tight situations.

The last tenet is indomitable spirit, an unconquerable attitude. Don't let anything get in your way, and don't let anything stop you from seeing the positive side of a situation. If somebody tells you that you can't do something, do it, whether it's landing that new kick, getting an A on a test in school, saving enough allowance money to buy something, or becoming a doctor. Nothing is impossible when your spirit cannot be dominated by negativity and hopelessness.

In our school, we talk about these tenets with both our child and adult classes, because our older students are going out into the community to be role models for the children they meet, and they need to be equipped with these traits as well.

We even go a step further and require these tenets be practiced and enforced before students can test for their next belt. Parents must sign a form that says their child is honoring these values on a daily basis at home, school, and everywhere else. This is another way we try to involve the entire community in raising bully-proofed children.

With their skills on the mat and by honoring the tenets, students feel as though they truly earn every single rank that they go through in martial arts. When they break a board, they break an obstacle. Nothing is handed to them with minimal effort, so when they walk away with that new achievement, they can feel their increased strength and confidence.

Working together is the only true way to eliminate bullying. The only way we're going to win this fight for our children is to join forces and make productive efforts as a whole community. It won't happen overnight and it requires big shifts in our thinking, as well as proactive and reactive solutions.

It's not enough to just talk about it. We must act, together.

Kimberly Tanny is the owner and head instructor of Tanny Academy of Martial Arts in Aurora, CO, where she teaches kids and adult martial arts classes as well as fitness kickboxing classes.

She is a 4th Degree Black Belt and International Instructor with the International Taekwon-do Federation. She has been training since 2001 and running Tanny Academy of Martial Arts since 2009.

Kimberly lives in Aurora, CO with her husband and two kids.

For more information, visit www.tannymartialarts.com.

CHAPTER 5:
"JUST IGNORE IT" AND OTHER MYTHS

BY CAROL CHAPMAN
RICHMOND, TEXAS

When children come to us about a bully, it's always tempting to dust off those go-to phrases that our parents used when we were growing up.

"Shrug it off."
"If what they're saying isn't true, then it doesn't matter."
"If you respond, they'll know they got a rise out of you."
"Stop being so sensitive. Ignore it."
"It's just kids being kids. They'll grow out it."

"Sticks and stones may break your bones, but words can never hurt you."

All of these sentiments operate under one massive misconception: that we, as humans, can turn our emotions on and off easily, as needed. A person who has never had to deal with bullying will have a hard time understanding why kids are especially bad at ignoring and dismissing them. Expecting them to do so naturally is totally unfeasible.

A lack of response isn't a guaranteed way for a child to protect themselves from bullying, anyway. Some bullies enjoy searching a person's face and body language for the smallest shred of evidence that what they're doing is working, which means that even walking away or avoidance can be a type of positive reinforcement. So how can we help?

It's gotten so much media attention in the last few years that parents and teachers know, without a doubt, that bullying is a problem children face every day. We've even worked pretty hard to nail down a proper definition of bullying, where both malicious intent and duration (or, in other words, a pattern of behavior) must be present.

Now, we must define what bullying looks like, so we don't miss it if it happens right in front of us. Many adults—maybe even children—envision the cliché picture of kids slamming each other into lockers and taking lunch money. But if you're reading this, you know it's far more varied than that.

Know Your Enemy

It's fine and good for adults to see a fight and break it up, because we know children should not fight, just like we know that children should not take one another's things, or call each other names, or tease one another. These types of bullying are easy to see and easy to correct in the moment.

But what about exclusion? What about children making each other feel as though they have no value and nothing to offer, as though they are worthless and unlikeable? How can we spot that subtle but devastating storm as it is brewing, and catch it early?

These days, kids are discouraged from being quiet and shy. Society encourages them to go outside and play with other children, to participate in class, and to make friends even if they'd rather keep to themselves in a corner reading a book. I was this way as a child, and there were other students at school who responded by excluding me and pretending I didn't exist. They went out of their way to make me feel like I didn't have any friends, and that my personality was the reason for it.

Thankfully, this forced me to turn my attention and focus to other things—like art and horseback riding—and to interact with people and groups outside of school. I became involved with the Future Farmers of America, an agricultural group, and even took on a leadership role within the club. Before I knew it, I was confidently standing on a stage, running some of the events and having a great time.

I no longer saw myself as a shy, quiet girl who was bullied for having no friends. It was hard to care what the kids at school thought of me, because I had other things going on that made me feel good about myself. I didn't need anyone's validation anymore.

Love Yourself & Protect Each Other

Children cannot control a bully's actions, but they can certainly make themselves a target by putting off vibes of low self-worth. Some kids may not stand up to bullies or say anything in response because they already don't feel great about themselves, and that can attract long-term patterns of malicious behavior from others that are impossible for them to ignore.

It has always been my goal, as a martial arts instructor, to teach the children in our community to be more confident, more disciplined, and more respectful. It is critical that children be allowed to discover their own value and find a variety of things that make them feel good about themselves. Not only do bullies not want to mess with someone who is self-reliant and confident, but if bullying does occur, a self-assured child will have an easier time tuning it out and dismissing it.

It may take a little while for a child to figure out a good response to a bully, and they should know that they have protection during that time. Becoming bullyproof starts with a feeling of safety and security at home. Children must know that they are always supported by a group of people who love them, and to whom they can reach out for reliable, reasonable backup as needed. They should know that their parents or guardians will assist them in whatever way is needed—physical protection, emotional comfort, and even by intervening if the situation calls for it. That will help them feel as though their physical safety and feelings are valued.

Teachers find themselves in an especially difficult position these days. Many can't effectively discipline kids, which means they can't deal with conflicts with as much flexibility as parents. Though teachers may not have a lot of power when it comes to actively punishing bullies, they are instrumental in creating a classroom environment that is inhospitable to patterns of malicious intent.

It takes a lot of nerve for an insecure child to speak up when there's a problem, so it's important that their concerns are listened to and that teachers are responsive during those conversations. Dismissing the problem or acting disinterested will convince the child that they are not valued enough to deserve help. After listening to the problem and showing gratitude to the child for pointing it out, teachers may then choose to send the other kid to the office, talk to the parents, or deal with it in a more benign way, like making the bully compliment each of the other kids in the class.

It's also helpful to create an environment where children recognize and celebrate one another's successes, to praise each other and to be excited about the progress of other students.

In one of our martial arts classes, we occasionally hold little races across the floor to warm up and have some fun. Regardless of who got there first or last, each student turns to the person next to them and gives them a high five, and says, "You did a great job." So many children struggle with the anger of not winning or coming in first place, so this may not come naturally to many of them at first. Soon, it becomes automatic. They're praising one another, and looking one another in the eye: "You are good. You did good."

It's a testament to children's capacity for kindness and cooperation that they can genuinely encourage each other while still maintaining that competitive spirit. Not only do they feel a decreased need to engage or join in with bullying behaviors, they are also helping one another gain the confidence they need to exude self-assurance, and creating small networks of support in the process. This ensures that bullies are left on the outskirts of the social circle, instead of controlling who gets to come in. Pretty soon, kids in such an environment will realize that they have nothing to gain by harming one another. That is bullyproofing at its finest.

Carol Chapman is the owner and head instructor at Fort Bend TaeKwonDo. Founded in 2010, the school has helped kids in Katy, Richmond, Fulshear, and Houston areas develop strength, focus, and confidence through traditional taekwondo.

Carol, a 5th Degree Black Belt and Level 4 nationally-certified instructor, began Taekwondo in 1997 at the "young" age of 30 after looking to find something challenging, motivating, and fun to get back in shape after her youngest began pre-school. One class was all it took before she was hooked and began her career in taekwondo. After earning her probationary black belt in 2000 at Fishers Martial Arts in Fishers, Indiana, Mrs. Chapman became a volunteer instructor and taught at Fishers Martial Arts until she and her family moved to the Katy area in 2009.

She opened Fort Bend TaeKwonDo in April, 2010 and continues to teach each class daily in addition to teaching at several area private schools for children with special needs.

Before becoming a school owner and while her 2 children were younger, Mrs. Chapman was actively involved with her son's Cub and Boy Scout troops and led her daughter's Girl Scout troop for 12 years. She served as a kindergarten teacher's aide and substitute teacher in the Carmel Clay School district as well as Gymboree Play teacher and manager of a mystery shopping company before moving to Katy.

For more information, visit www.fortbendtkd.com.

CHAPTER 6: DIFFERENT PROBLEMS, DIFFERENT SOLUTIONS

BY J.P. DO
IRVINE, CALIFORNIA

Being bullied as a child made me who I am today, but not in the way you might expect. I remember one instance in particular that really put me on the road to my future. I was on the playground, playing with my friends and minding my own business, when some older children announced that they were going to take over the court. They pushed us off the side, roughly, in a manner that really physically threatened us.

Like every child who gets bullied, I responded emotionally. I was very upset, and I couldn't stop asking myself what I could do to protect myself from ever being treated like that again. That's when I decided to ask my parents to put me in martial arts. I was about ten years old.

My parents' support empowered me to take this step, which would end up being critical to my development and my happiness in life. They were very excited about me going into martial arts, because they knew I needed a way to develop my confidence and self-assurance.

That support is what every child needs to take important steps in their lives, and especially to become bully-proof.

However, me learning martial arts was not the end of my need to protect myself. What happened to me as a younger child still stuck with me, and as I developed my self-defense skills, I found myself constantly running a variety of bullying situations in my head just to make absolutely certain that I would know exactly what to do when it was time to do it.

It was all to my benefit, however. There were a few more incidents that arose in my life where I needed physical protection, and martial arts gave me the tools I needed to defend myself quickly and effectively, and get away from tight situations safely. Having the basic knowledge, given to me by my martial arts training, helped me turn my nervousness and anxiety into power and confidence.

I've been doing martial arts for 25 years, now. I'm a fifth-degree black belt, and I opened ATA Irvine—my Taekwondo school—over 10 years ago. I've seen bullying in almost all of its forms through working with my young students, and with parents and adults and teachers. Bullying has certainly changed quite a bit since I was a little kid on that playground getting shoved around by the other children.

When we dealt with bullying back in the day, it was much more physically involved. Bullying was generally considered to be threat to your body and your nerves. However, kids these days have taken it to a whole different level. In many ways, bullying of the body has been retired and replaced with full-on bullying of a person's psyche, through social media, manipulation, verbal harassment, and exclusion.

While they are both unacceptable, if I had to choose between the two—physical bullying and psychological bullying—I was say that the psychological strategy that bullies today have undertaken is worse. With physical bullying, you can clearly *see* your opponent. You can size them up based on their physical demeanor, muscles, bone structure, etc, and you can train yourself to defend against whatever is thrown at you. Then you can see the evidence of your efforts in whether or not they stumble backwards, come at you again, or leave your presence entirely, and you can immediately adjust your technique accordingly, if you have the training to do so.

However, there are dangerous mysteries involved with psychological bullying. Even if you can look the other person in the eye, you have no way of knowing what they're capable of or what they're going to throw at you. Worst of all, there are ways that psychological bullying can happen anonymously, which makes the victim feel that much more helpless, because they can't even see their attacker through the smokescreen of technology. That's why bullying seems so much more extreme these days than it did when I was a child.

There's that old saying that says, "Stick and stones can break your bones, but words can never hurt me," but when you get pushed around on the playground—even when you get hit—those wounds will heal. However, the attacks on a person's psychological state can last far longer. Adding insult to injury, there is often a larger audience to cyber-bullying and social media humiliation—sometimes hundreds of people—which puts a magnifying glass on a child's pain for the world to see.

Despite increased coverage of really extreme bullying situations, and despite the good intentions of hundreds of bullying awareness programs across the country, there are still people out there who say that bullying isn't really a big problem anymore. Those are people who think that bullying has to involve kids physically assaulting one another. Since that is not the primary mode of bullying anymore—since that's not what we *see*—they think it's not an issue.

This "out of sight, out of mind" approach is, unfortunately, exactly the view that bullies want us to have. They want to be invisible, so we have to look that much harder at the facts, at the percentage of children that commit suicide or undertake other drastic measures because they are bullied in ways that are invisible to most adults.

One of the big place where bullying happens is at school. Kids spend a lot of time there, and these days, there might be more than 20 kids for every adult there is in the classroom. We all know that teachers care about their students, but their primary role is to educate.

Some schools have what's called a zero-tolerance rule, which says that any fighting at all should be punished, no matter who was at fault. I think that's helpful, to a degree, because children need to understand that resorting to physical assault is unacceptable, and will be punished. It's a decent deterrent. However, what's more important is educating everyone involved—the bully, the person being bullied, and the teacher—and reminding them that communication is a more effective way of solving conflict than violence.

Rather than punishment, the real focus should be on prevention. Holding bully-prevention classes and workshops is a good place to start, and I believe that offering bully-support groups and providing easy access to counselors is important as well. My parents' support made me strong as a child, and every child deserves to know that there are adults who have their back, adults who can be trusted, adults who want to hear about any situation that has made the child feel threatened.

Teachers, support staff, and even other students should all be included in these endeavors, to reinforce with everyone that bully-prevention is everyone's responsibility. Adults should pay particular attention to how the children respond to bully-proofing efforts, because, just like anything else, if the kids are not engaged in what you're teaching, they aren't going to internalize it the way they should for it to be effective. There are programs out there with great content that's delivered in such a boring way that it'd be nearly impossible for children to get anything out of it. Some strategies for engagement definitely include the instructor's tone of voice, the way they carry themselves and their message, whether or not they have personal experience or stories to share, and how well they can really get to the core of the issue.

It's also important to understand your audience. Talking to elementary-school kids is different from talking to high-schoolers, as we all know. Younger children require more interaction and hands-on learning, while older children sometimes do better with conversation.

I've taught anti-bullying techniques to children as young as seven. The earlier they are introduced to these concepts, the better, because younger children absorb more information quicker than older kids. They have an easier time incorporating new skills with what they already know in ways that will allow them to carry those ideas forward into their futures.

And because bullying tactics are different amongst the age groups, the content should change as well. For younger kids, it's sometimes enough to discuss the importance of telling an adult whenever they feel uncomfortable, threatened, or bullied. For older kids—11-year olds to teenagers—I would definitely discuss social media etiquette. For example, they should know it's not okay to post a picture of their friends (or anybody) in a bad situation. It's not okay to point fingers publicly at a friend (or anybody) in a way that can never be taken back. They need to learn how to ask themselves, in everything they do online, whether it is something they would want done to them in return.

Now, we've talked a lot about bully-proofing efforts outside of the home, but the parents pay an even more critical role in their child's life when it comes to reinforcing education and offering support. It's important that parents be held accountable for these responsibilities. They should be present at the bully-proofing seminars. They should sign the waivers when it's time to do so. They should seek out their own training that will allow them to serve their children in these roles. I've long thought there should be a separate set of classes for the parents to attend, that will empower them to be supportive of their children in ways that will make them bully-proof.

For example, if a parent came to me asking what they should do about their child being bullied at school, I would tell them that keeping open lines of communication with their child is the best place to start. Their child should feel absolutely no hesitation in coming to them and saying, "I have a problem, and I'd like your help in solving it." That mutual trust is going to give parents an open door to help their child whenever their help is needed.

And, of course, learning to stand up to and defend against bullies is something taught in all martial-arts classes, making it an exceptional extra-curricular activity for the family that truly wants to become bully-proof. At ATA Irvine, we teach martial-art techniques that are centuries old in ways that are engaging and relevant to the changing world our kids live in. We are not interested in just teaching self-defense, but also in nurturing the complete personal development of each student. These are good things to look for when choosing a martial-arts program that's right for your child.

J.P. Do is a martial arts instructor in the American Taekwondo Association. He has been practicing martial arts for over 25 years.

J.P. finds Teaching the life skills of respect, integrity, and focus while reinforcing the martial art aspect is a true blessing. He couldn't imagine doing anything else as his career.

J.P. looks forward to every day being able to put a smile on his students' faces while teaching then self defense and self confidence.

For more information, visit www.atairvine.com

CHAPTER 7: MAKE SUPERHEROES, NOT VICTIMS

BY LUIS JIMENEZ
EDNA, TEXAS

Some adults get really uncomfortable and offended when I tell them that kids these days get their feelings hurt easier than kids in the 80's and 90's. No one wants to believe that their child might be more fragile now than they would have been in a different generation, but I believe that every kid can become a bully-proof superhero. I wouldn't do what I do if I doubted that for an instant.

I'm the owner of Zen Martial Arts in Edna, Texas. My son Joey, who is six years old, is at the karate school all the time, listening and learning just like everyone else. He's constantly absorbing instructions on what to do and what not to do about bullies, and he knows the right steps to take. However, when he was bullied in his first year of school, he was just a little too unsure and shy to go through with them. It goes to show that even the people who know what to do in theory can have a hard time putting it into practice. I had a similar problem, many years ago.

When I was in junior high, there were three or four bullies who always roamed around in a pack, calling people names. I was a blue belt in karate at the time, but they didn't know that, so they picked on me nonstop for over a year. I ignored and avoided them as much as I could until they were especially cruel to me in recess one day.

I said, "That's it. No more. I'm not going to take it anymore. After school, we're going to go around the school and we're just going to settle this."

Boy, did we settle it. One of my friends and I started a fight with them that lasted all of about two seconds. One of the guys swung at me, and the next thing I knew, I was on top of him, punching wildly as a teacher dragged me off. My friend told me how awesome it was to see me fly into a rage and handle my business.

The very next day he saw me at school, he just turned around and went the other way. I was never bullied again in school.

I'm now a sixth-degree black belt in karate-do, a third-degree black belt in kickboxing, and I've been a sparring world champion eight times. You'd think I'd be proud of what I did when I was a kid to stand up for myself.

However, I knew then, as I know now, that I wasn't grappling on a mat with gloves and pads on. This was violence, plain and simple, and going into a zone like that was scary. That kid really didn't deserve that black eye if there was anything else I could've done to end the behavior. It was a solution that solved the problem, but it was also a solution that should've been a last resort, not a first one. I'm not proud of it.

Of course that sort of altercation would not be tolerated by any school in 2017, even though bullying has (in many ways) gotten worse since then. Now bullies often hide behind their phone, their keyboards, their iPads. They don't say things to other kids' faces anymore, but the words cut the same as they ever have.

My theory is that children have their feelings hurt easier these days because we're a society that's decided to create victims instead of up-standers.

In school, we teach kids that if they get into any kind of situation—offensive or defensive, whether they're the bully or the bullied—they will have to answer to the principal, or with suspension or detention.

Young parents with kids contribute to this mindset as well. There's nothing wrong with trying to build a bubble for you and your family; that's the ultimate goal for all of us. However, if your child is in a public school, it's not going to happen, so go ahead and forget all of those feel-good phrases you tell yourself when you want to ignore what might be happening during school hours: "It can happen to somebody else, but it's not happening to my kid," or "My kid is strong enough to say no," or, "He's not going to be bullied because he's so cool and popular," or "No one would hurt my kid because (s)he's so cute and sweet."

So if children are being told at school that defending themselves is a bad thing, and they're being told at home that their problems can't exist, what have you created? A victim.

Victims aren't going to say anything. They're just going to take it. They're going to hang their heads, walk away from bullies, and take on the impossible burden of trying to just ignore it. Their inner dialogue won't be, "I am my own person, and I deserve to walk through the halls and down the sidewalks unafraid." Instead they'll say to themselves, "I don't want to get in trouble. I don't want to disappoint my parents. I don't want this to affect my school, my grades, my academic records. I won't say anything."

They don't feel comfortable saying to their guardian, "I'm having a problem at school. Can you please help me figure out what to do?" That unwillingness to voice their pain creates a rift between the child and the adults in their lives. Of course, that silence becomes even more dangerous once they have a phone in their hands and computers at their disposal. They will take whatever bullies dish out, because they don't want to be snitches. They don't want to be the kid that cries to Mommy.

When I was in junior high, it took me a year to finally stand up for myself. For kids today, it may take even longer, or never, to plainly display behaviors that alert adults to their situation. At that point—after they've been kicked, punched, called names, mugged, and spit on—it is often too late to easily break that cycle.

We cannot keep teaching children that bullying is a normal part of their everyday lives. We cannot keep advocating silence. We cannot keep creating victims, because the numbers and percentages associated with bullying are only going up every year. More and more kids are getting involved in martial art activities in my school because they've been bullied, so I cover it as a part of an intro class that every student in my school takes whether they're bullied or not. In it, we discuss the definition of bullying and go over the things that you can and shouldn't say to bullies.

I teach the following: Say no. Put your hands in front of you. Say stop, really loudly. Don't just use your voice, but your body language as well. When you tell the bully to stop, everyone around should hear you declaring this threat to your wellbeing, even the teachers.

The behaviors probably won't stop immediately, but teaching kids that they *can* stand up for themselves in a productive way is a huge step in creating up-standers instead of victims.

Most of the kids at my school being bullied are targets because they walk, talk, look, and act like the victims we discussed earlier. They're being attacked because their physique and body language makes them appear fragile and breakable, which are qualities that bullies love in a victim.

The physical exercises in martial arts strengthen their bodies, and they can't help but carry themselves differently, secure in the knowledge that they can block a punch if they need to. We teach the kids that they may not be Superman, but they are a person who deserves to be safe and happy, and a person who is capable of protecting themselves.

Martial arts also gives kids yet another set of adults and friends who will have their backs and be supportive if they need to be firm with a bully, because it's never okay to walk away from someone who is constantly hurting you. That will only make things worse—

way worse—because now the bully knows he has power over you, and he's going to seek you out even more. He'll look for you behind the school, on the playground, at the movies, and at the mall, and we all know what happens next.

It's also never okay to walk away from a person who is being bullied. Kids are told to never intervene in a fight, which is why we suddenly have all these videos on the internet of two kids fighting or a kid being bullied. There's one kid suffering, a few kids doing the bullying, and then ten kids standing around with their phones recording what's going on. That's a shame.

Bullying is like an illness. Ignoring or glorifying an illness won't cure it.

Because bullying is a repetitive behavior designed to hurt someone, we unfortunately have to wait until it happens a second time to really determine if that's what it is. But if a child pushes another child on purpose or asks them for money even once, the bullied parties should be able to report those behaviors so they can be documented immediately. That way, if one kid is engaging in the same negative behavior with multiple students, a teacher has all the information they need to say, "This wasn't an accident. This is a pattern, and it needs to be addressed now. "

One child effectively standing up to a bully probably won't transform the bully into a solid citizen. In fact, they're more likely to just go hunting for another victim. Bullies are usually being bullied at home somehow—verbally, physically, psychologically—so in my opinion, bullies need help to make the behaviors stop. Counseling would be a good option, but I've heard of very few bullies actually following through with that sort of treatment.

They need to know that being a bully is not cool. It is not going to make you popular. It's going to make you a person that other people don't want to be around, and if you have friends, you're not going to have them for very long.

If a parent has the awareness and honesty to admit their kid is a bully, they need to start looking for a place where the child can find discipline, structure, and a way to take his or her anger and energy out. Martial arts could change a bully's life. It's a place to throw punches and kicks without hurting anyone, and a place to take punches and kicks to know what it feels like. In a controlled environment—with pads and gloves and a supervisor—that bully will eventually know the anxiety that comes with sparring against a bigger kid or even an adult. That offers a much-needed reality check, and builds empathy as well.

The first step in raising a bully-proof child really is just talking to them. Have conversations with them. You don't have to ask rapid-fire questions all the time to know what's going on at school. Ask them about their friends, and who they hang out with at school. Make it clear that you acknowledge their experiences outside of the house, and if something happens, you want and need to hear about it.

The second step is to make sure they understand that it is okay to set boundaries for themselves, and to enforce those boundaries with a strong voice and confident body language that simply says, "Stop." No punches necessary.

The third step is to make very clear that fear and nervousness and doubt are all emotions that exist, but they are all emotions that can be controlled. Any child or adult who can really control their negative and positive emotions to make themselves more resilient is a true sensei, a true master.

Let's stop bullying. Let's make kids into up-standing superheroes.

6th Degree in Karatedo,

3rd Degree in Kickboxing

8 times Sparring World champion

Started Martial Arts in 1983

Owner of Zen Martial Arts in Edna, Texas since 2010

Father of Blair & Joey

For more information, visit www.zenma.org.

CHAPTER 8:
THE MINECRAFT LESSONS

BY LISA PIPER
MCDONOUGH, GEORGIA

Today, parents and teachers alike have to deal with the phenomenon knows as Minecraft.

It's an amazingly simple concept, and at first it makes no sense as to why kids love it so much. Players build their buildings in this virtual world, pixel by pixel. It's like a digital Legoland. Kids can play this game for hours on their xBox, or iPad, or sit on YouTube watching videos of *other kids playing Minecraft.*

But with a little more investigation, the reason why kids love this is surprisingly clear: it's an arena that players can manipulate their world, and feel the sense of achievement through "leveling up."

Video games typically enhance a player's strengths and minimize their weaknesses. So a player has a very different persona in the videogame world than they do in the real world. For many people who play video games, who often give themselves the title "gamer," this is an easy and compelling escape from the reality of life.

As a martial artist, some of the things we talk about in training is the importance of building your confidence, but also understanding what your strengths are, what your vulnerabilities are and work on those. Nothing builds self-esteem than to do things for yourself and understand what your vulnerabilities are, it can also work on life and self-improvement. Enhancing your skills, enhancing how you see yourself and enhancing your position in the world, with your friends, your family, your community. All in real life.

As a kid, I faced real-life challenges in school. I was very different than anyone else in my community. I was raised in a primarily white community, in Jonesboro, Georgia. And it was a little outside of Atlanta, so a lot of my friends had very different families and cultures that were very different from mine. So, you know, often people would find easy ways to poke fun at it and say things that hurt me, and maybe undermine some of the things I thought about myself.

As a child, I started martial arts and through that I was able to build up my different levels of self-respect and respect for others and work on my self-esteem and teaching me how to become self-reliant and independent. And I was able to really build up my confidence so that I saw the world very differently and was able to learn how to bully-proof myself. Today I get to do the same thing for today's youth.

A lot of parents bring their children to us because they want the child to learn confidence and also to be more respectful at home, at school, throughout the community. But in teaching those very same things, you're teaching them to see the world differently as well and respond to it, and position themselves with their friends, with their family, in society and to the world in a stronger manner. To bully-proof themselves.

This is especially important today, as bullying really has changed. The nature and methods are much different than when many of today's parents went through it like I did. Society has shifted, especially with technology.

If you look at the impact that technology has had on us as a people, it made bullying into a societal issue. It transcends age, it transcends gender, transcends different cultures. It's a societal issue. And technology has a very big impact on our society. With boundaries well-drawn, technology does help us in life and our productivity. However, when the advantages are gone, and we star to focus only on what feels good, we start losing track of the impact technology has on life.

Our aggression goes up. Our anxiety levels increase. Kids that are playing video games, they become more and more aggressive. They're in a world that caters completely just to them.

This affects adults too. People start to believe they're the center of the world—because in a video game, that is exactly the case.. And then they get out of the video game and now they're in reality, and they have the same expectations of being catered-to that the electronics does. So they aren't as patient, aren't as tolerant; lack impulse control. They often expect immediate gratification.

We're in a very different world than in the 70s and 80s when many of today's parents were in childhood. Kids are now being raised with (and in some cases, *by*) technology. Key life skills that many adults developed while growing up in a non-technologically saturated world may be missing for kids today. This includes traits like patience and tolerance and our ability to overcome setbacks and struggles, and push through challenges to make things happen in our lives.

The Fine Line

One of the things we talk about in the martial arts program is that technology is a great thing to have. It's going stay forever. It is also very important to define *where it should be in our lives* and *how it should be in our lives* and the boundaries that we need to set for it.

One thing we tell our parents, I said first of all, with bullying not only being for children, it continues to adulthood and it's really important to get a hold of understanding how to become bully-proof in real life to have a life of happiness. We tell our parents to have only certain times when technology is allowed and allow only so often during the week, because kids really start actually having the mindset of thinking life is like the technology, rather than understanding that they have to learn, negotiate and be able to deal with setbacks and struggles. Things that are not necessarily how they are in the videogame world. They need to learn that reality is a very different life and sometimes, those two worlds kind of get mixed up and it helps if parents draw boundaries for that. Part of a parent's role is to define these boundaries for children.

For example, in martial arts, we talk about building your confidence, building your self-esteem; leveling up your respect for what you do for yourself, and the level of respect you have for yourself; and also levels of respect you have for others so you can build a world of family, friends and support for yourself. These are things you can't do in videogames, because the video game is already there so therefore you don't realize the importance of it.

This works in the community and in local schools, with scout groups, parents and families. We teach the importance of helping children understand their place in this world: in terms of their confidence; how to work on their strengths and vulnerabilities; and develop skills to overcome challenges and struggles. And especially to level up their respect for themselves and others.

The Minecraft World

A lot of kids talk about Minecraft because that's a huge game with them, and we can use the game as a common platform to teach life skills. So we use the technology reference because that's what kids relate to most quickly and easily, and really helps the information hit home. You have to build, you have to invest and sometimes videogames, there's no creativity in building and investing – it's just there and you basically manipulate it. But life is very different in that you have to build things and grow things.

In life, you build your relationships with people, yourself, and building your skills. You have to level up your place in this world. You have to level up how you look at yourself at all times. In video games, you're always going from one level to the next. When teaching life skills, we use the leveling-up in videogames in the same way. We talk about a ladder and how they level up all the different things in their lives is very important: how they level up their performance in school; how they level up the relationships at home with Mom and Dad, and their brothers and sisters; how to level up themselves in connection with who they are and standing up for who they are.

They have to literally build their world. It's just like Minecraft, in terms of building up your world, but it's not in bricks and pixels and colors – it's actually in relationships and people that we talk to and learn from. We learn to compromise on our relationships and build them up and remember the people in our lives. We practice social interaction, building healthy boundaries and understanding healthy relationships with those in our world.

So that's kind of what we talk about. Some people think that martial arts is just about physical conflict with others and fighting. That is one aspect of it. Martial arts is also about the conflict within yourself, building yourself up, and growing as an individual. This in turn helps to teach how to build other people up, so that you have strong teams in your life and the support in your life.

Bullying in Schools

One of the key areas of influence for children in developing these life skills is at schools. Children will spend 6-8 hours a day at school, typically 180 days a year. Oftentimes this is an intimate setting with the same group of kids in a classroom, and they get to know one another quite well. This can be both helpful and harmful in terms of bullying.

This being said, teaching appreciation and respect for others is vitally important to teach kids to become bullyproof. While bullying, in itself, may never be completely eradicated, we can still reduce the harmful effects on kids through education. This must include: teaching people what bullying is; and how to handle bullying if and when it occurs.

One of the sections of our bully prevention courses, is to talk about the difference between "name calling," and when a situation escalates to something that must be reported. This way, teachers have a basis from which to take care of their students at different levels of escalation that happen. Clearly, "name calling" will be handled differently than a violent situation.

Of course, prevention and avoidance is the best defense against bullying. For example, when you first have a kindergarten class coming into school, the focus can be placed on the individual in terms of respect, confidence and self-esteem. It also is important to understand their self-value and develop relationships. This allows kids to learn not to simply tolerate negative behavior from peers, but had to draw boundaries and walk away from it.

The way this can be taught in school, as well as how we do this in martial arts, can start with the body. Body language affects the way kids feel about themselves. Teach kids to stand tall, which is leads to confident body language. When they feel this certain way about themselves, that they are confident, they aren't affected so acutely when bullies try to pick on them. In fact, the more confident kids tend to be picked on *less*.

When a child knows who they are, they know that they have vulnerabilities, and they know they have their own strengths, they can work on developing both. This helps build the confidence and assurance that no matter what their vulnerabilities are (which is what typically bullies will look at), they're able to overcome them and move forward. Pair that along with the realization that *everybody has their own vulnerabilities, not just you.* When children are taught kindness and respect, they can also be empowered to choose positive, constructive behavior that helps others. When a kid sees another child's vulnerabilities, they choose how to interact. Just because a bully chooses to exploit and take advantage of another kid's weaknesses, they don't have to. How a bully chooses to address someone's vulnerabilities is not how they have to. They can be someone very different and they can be a leader who helps enhance their friends, grow relationships, and develop and appreciate people.

As a teacher (whether at schools or in any leadership position), the more you're talking about that, the more people will learn to become bullyproofed and develop those around them, to become a leader. Be more than just be a part of a group, but to be someone who wants and enhances those around them. If a teacher can build that synergy in a room, then they really are definitely building an environment that's not tolerant to bullying but to really help others improve and grow.

The Bullyproof Mindset

When looking at bullying, while behavior is important, the *mindset* behind the behavior is key. When this is addressed in kids, you can have long-term behavioral change. In terms of schools, a typical response to bullying is, "Johnny bullied Sue, so let's just bring Sue up to Johnny and make Johnny apologize to her." While this most often *does* result in an apology from the bully, there often is no real shift in the mindset from which the bullying stemmed from. The end result is that there is an *increase* in conflict, rather than the decrease.

Conflict simply leads to more conflict, which shows up in different ways, both negative. First, the child who was the target of bullying may in turn start to show bullying behavior, because that is the kind of behavior that they see is accepted. Second, bullies themselves may continue their negative behavior because it is reinforced: they are getting the attention they seek, not just from their target, but also from the teachers. These two, paired together, create a downward spiral of bullying behavior in the classroom.

Instead, a teach can bring the two kids together, find something that they have in common, and being able to build off of that. Find things that you can appreciate in one another. Showing love and understanding is key. Bullies aren't bullies because they hate people, or don't like them. *They're bullying because they have problems and issues of their own that need to be taken care of.* There's a lack of understanding, and so to force people to apologize to one another and speak to them in a way that the teacher is asking them to, does not help bullying, but creates more situations for someone to want to bully because now there's retaliation and revenge that has to happen. It's more about learning and finding ways to show commonality between the two and building a relationship, and including teaching people who bully how to include others and the positive aspects of including others.

Understanding The Difference: Simple Conflict, or Bullying?

So what exactly is the difference between true "bullying" and simple interpersonal conflicts that children have? Many definitions include the following:

1) Negative intent. The person who is the "bully" *intentionally* does things or says things to hurt another person.

2) Frequency. The person who is the "bully" shows a pattern of this behavior, either with a single target (Johnny continually targets Sue) or multiple targets (Johnny shows the same bullying behavior to Sue, Billy, and Jesse)

There is, however, a third and important consideration, which is an *imbalance of power.* Conflicts between kids is quite normal. However, when a kid uses some imbalance of power: whether it be physical strength, embarrassing information, or popularity among peers to isolate a kid who isn't popular; this is when it becomes true bullying.

When talking to kids who are bullied, people sometimes have "bully moments." They may say things that are hurtful, and not realize it. This is one example of a situation when using "countering words" would be appropriate. The target of the bullying may use the "rubber band" technique to throw off the person. For example, "Yeah, I've heard that before!" or "You're trying to make fun of me?" are taught in several anti-bully programs.

Oftentimes, that kind of knowledge can help children deal with conflicts at school. It's at this point that "walking away" can be an effective solution, because the person who initiated the "bullying behavior" is disarmed.

Understanding Bullies, and Proactive Prevention

If your kid is bullied, you can ask them, "Do people bully you because there really is something wrong with you?" The answer is simply, "no." It's important to teach children that there is nothing wrong with them, but all people have vulnerabilities that they need to work on. Furthermore, with kids it is important to teach them that vu*lnerability is the thing that makes you special. It sets them apart.*

When someone says mean things to your child, or does mean things, sometimes they're having a "bully moment." They're lashing out at someone else, because of something going on within themselves, whether that person deserves it or not.

The key is to start as early as possible, to prevent the behaviors of bullies from affecting kids. These are lessons like avoiding people who have bully issues, showing body language and strength in themselves, and walking strong and tall. Teach kids to create good habits in your life that build them up and make them stronger. Give kids an example of peers who are good people to make friends with, so they can build that support team. So then when bullying happens they know exactly who you can go to for help and who you can talk to.

Building Kids Up One Level at a Time

This chapter started by talking about Minecraft. What is so interesting is the number of parallels between a video game, and raising kids to be bullyproof.

Build up a kid's confidence and respect, block by block, bit by bit, little by little from the beginning level of kindergarten (or as soon as possible!)

Surround yourself with other friendly players who will be a good support team in case of challenges.

And if you need help getting to the next level, there is always someone who has worked this stage before. Many communities have events in their local area where they teach different strategies on becoming bullyproof, how to deal with negative behaviors at school, and what parents can do to empower their kids.

The bottom line is, start early. If parents need help with bullying, there are lots of resources in communities that are valuable and can help. Five minutes with someone can really help enhance a kid's ability to feel good about themselves, but also to be able to be stronger and have the shield up, so when bullying happens, they know how to take care of it. And truly level up their life!

Lisa Piper is a Nationally Certified ATA 5th Degree Black Belt instructor, competition judge, and National Judge. She is a two-time recipient of the Grand Master H.U. Lee Instructor's Special Merit Award. In the ATA Instructor Certification Camp, Lisa achieved a perfect score 100 in the written exam and finished in the top 3% of the squad leadership workouts, and was the youngest in her class.

Being in the ATA since 1982, Lisa has been active in the ATA World Tournament Circuit and has ranked in the Top Ten and even the Top Four qualifying to compete for World Champion for every year as a 1st degree up until 5th degree. Lisa has taught several self-defense seminars for women and kids throughout the state of Georgia.

Lisa has partnered with several organizations to further grow and empower herself and the citizens of our community through martial arts, bully prevention, bully defense, conflict resolution, motivation, and personal growth such as Kidz N Power, Code Amber, Safety Net Kids, Olweus, and HYPER.

Lisa is a graduate from Georgia State University in Business Management. She takes her responsibilities seriously as a role model, especially for young students, teaching them the importance of having strong minds, strong bodies and the important lifelong skill of always learning.

For more information, visit www.ata-bba.net.

CHAPTER 9: BEING PROACTIVE AND GETTING EDUCATED

BY JOHNNIE MORRIS
EL CAJON, CALIFORNIA

Bullying is something that touches almost everyone at some point in their lives, whether it's through personal experience or seeing a loved one face the challenges associated with having a bully. As a child I was bullied myself and understand how difficult it can be for kids who are going through it. As the owner and Chief Instructor of Aspire Martial Arts in California I've made it my goal to help as many kids become as bullyproof as possible and I'm looking forward to sharing some thoughts in this book.

Is Bullying Really a Problem?

This is a question I get asked a lot. Often it's by parents who either aren't sure if they should be concerned about existing behavior they're finding out about or who are worried about the potential for bullying to happen to their kids at school. As I already mentioned, bullying is something that will affect nearly everyone in some way. Because of this it's my opinion that yes, bullying really is a problem - one that deserves focus and attention in order to combat it.

Part of the problem I find with bullying is the way it tends to get swept under the rug until it's too late. On the one hand you could say that there are lots of news stories about bullying lately and that coverage about bullying is more prevalent in the media today than it's been in years past. All of this is true, but on the other hand we really only hear about bullying after the fact, after something tragic has happened. I'd like to focus on what happens *before* the tragedies and try to prevent bullying events from happening in the first place. With all of the technology and social media we have available now I think that there's a real potential to increase awareness and be proactive in order to lessen the tragic events we hear about so often. I don't think this solution will be able to eliminate bullying entirely because it's something that will always be around in some form, but I do think that we can get the number of incidents down much lower.

Be Proactive

Being proactive in the fight against bullying is something we can all do, and the first step is to be as educated as possible when it comes to bullying. By being educated I mean do as much research as you can in order to form your own opinion about what bullying is and what it means to you. There are so many resources available today including online research, community groups, PTA groups, and local seminars. Once you have an idea about your own beliefs on bullying it's amazing how easy you'll be able to find supporting materials and ways to continue your education.

Another step to being proactive is being committed. Doing research or attending a single seminar about bullying isn't cause to pat yourself on the back and assume your job is done. As a parent trying to help your child become bullyproof you need to take that information and do something with it. You also need to continue seeking out new information and implementing it in your home so you'll be proactive in the fight against bullying. It will be much easier on you and your children if you engage in the process early and continue it as opposed to starting and stopping only when issues arise.

How to Get Educated

I mentioned that local seminars and groups are great ways to familiarize yourself with bullying and start to work on bullyproofing your kids. When seeking out different programs there are certainly a fair number of quality programs, but there are also some that aren't worth your time. If you're looking to find a quality resource to help your quest for bullyproofing there are some key elements to consider. First, did the program you're looking into come from a direct referral? Often those are the best because you'll be able to hear about someone's actual experience. You should also find out how long the program has been around, and if their up to date on any certifications or training that might be pertinent. Another big element to consider is if they're well versed on different types of bullying and if they'll be going over the different types in their presentation. There are many types of bullying including physical, verbal, cyber, and even teen and adult issues like bullies in the workplace. It's best to get some information about each of these areas, but it's especially important to find out what areas will be covered if there is a specific one that pertains to your situation in particular.

Individual Strategies

While finding a group or seminar that focuses on bullyproofing is a great strategy, there are also a number of things you can be doing in the meantime to help your child become bullyproof. One of the most important things you can do is focus on building confidence in your child so they have the ability to stand up for themselves if needed. Confidence is the number one deterrent of bullies because they'll almost always seek out weaker victims. If your child walks with their head down, speaks quietly, or can't tell someone to leave them alone then they may be a target.

My own issues with bullying were due to a lack of confidence and that's one of the reasons I recommend martial arts as an activity for any kids, but especially those who have confidence or self-esteem issues. I can say with 100% certainty that I'm a product of being bullyproof through martial arts because I gained the confidence I needed to not get picked on anymore. Just one example of how martial arts builds confidence is by working with someone who's bigger than you. If a child is working out with a kid who's bigger than them in the dojo and they see that they can hold their own then that builds up confidence in them. That transfers to a situation that may come up in school, and instead of being afraid they have enough confidence to stand up to a bully even if they're bigger. Again, this is just one of many examples of how martial arts can help with things like confidence, self-esteem, goal setting, and more. Martial arts may not be the right solution for everyone, but I can honestly say that I wouldn't be the person I am today without martial arts and I think it's something that all kids could benefit from.

Things That Don't Work

With so much information available about bullying thee days I think that one thing that happens is a lot of misinformation gets spread. One of the biggest mistakes I See with how people are handling bullying right now comes down to two three words - "just ignore it". These three words are often told to kids who are being bullied as advice for what to do, and in my opinion it's one of the worst things we can tell kids. Bullies look for weakness, and a victim who will just let them get away with anything they want is a prime target. If a kid comes to you looking for advice it's because they don't know what to do, and telling them to just ignore it is almost the same as telling them to get lost because you don't care. That's not what you mean, but essentially that's what your advice amounts to. Instead, take the time to listen to exactly what is going on and try to come up with realistic solutions that will last. Again, it comes down to seeking out information so you can be educated and ready to deal with these situations.

"Just ignore it" isn't a phrase isolated to parents, though. Unfortunately it's also being used in many school systems. Some school systems actively choose to ignore bullying behavior as a way to avoid legal issues. They're afraid that if they acknowledge the behavior then they're opening themselves up to more issues than they want. Other times schools just ignore bullying because they lack the proper training and education to deal with it, and oftentimes aren't even able to recognize when behavior goes from bothersome to bullying. Again it comes down to being educated about bullying and taking a proactive approach to nip it in the bud before it leads to tragedy.

Limit What Can't Be Eliminated

While we're probably never going to eliminate bullying from the world completely we can and should do what we can to limit its effects, meaning that while there still might be bullying we can take kids and make them confident so they're much less likely to be bullied. It's not a process that will come quick or easy, but it will certainly be well worth it. I encourage anyone reading this book to take the next step by finding some type of activity or community group that focuses on bullyproofing strategies and learn as much as you can. Bullying isn't going away anytime soon, but with parents armed with knowledge and children armed with confidence we can work together to make the next generation as bullyproof as possible.

Johnnie Morris is the owner and instructor at Aspire Martial Arts in El Cajon, California. A long-time practitioner of Taekwondo, Johnnie has made it his passion and career to teach and inspire his students to be empowered and strong people.

For more information, visit www.aspireata.com

GETTING INVOLVED WITH THE BULLYPROOF PROJECT

The *Bullyproof: Unleash the Hero Inside Your Kid* book series is designed to raise awareness. However, awareness isn't enough. To effect true, lasting change in our communities, it requires action.

The contributing authors of the *Bullyproof* series are committed to bettering their hometowns through community involvement. Many are on speaking tours, school visits, or hold bullyproof classes. They are known as the Bully Experts in their town, the go-to source of real transformation in people.

The truth is that one can't read a book, or take one workshop, or attend one pep rally and become bullyproof. It takes time, effort, energy and commitment.

These contributing authors have missions in their businesses to help kids and adults become empowered, and the best way for them is to establish an ongoing working relationship with their clients and communities.

If you, like them, are completely committed to transforming your community and making it bullyproof, and you would like to be involved in a future volume of the *Bullyproof: Unleash the Hero Inside Your Kid* series, then we should talk.

Contact us at www.bullyproofamerica.org or via email at info@bullyproofamerica.org and let's make a difference in our communities *together*.

Made in the USA
Monee, IL
02 November 2023

45622331R00066